To Lewis, Wilf, Daniel, Thea, Davina, Danae, Aiden, Bess and Zara

Dear World Leaders

A response to children's letters about climate change

Aled Jones

Illustrators:

Tabitha Wall
(cover & plants and animals)

Ridley Green
(climate change & jobs)

Maria Luísa *(people & home)*

Summer Wilson *(energy)*

Isobel Johnson
(transport & community)

Abigail Challis
(forests & behaviour)

Tess Duffin *(food)*

Abi Winter *(waste)*

Samantha Stroud *(leadership)*

Excerpts from the following children's letters were used to inspire the illustrations:

Jason *(Nigeria)*

Elliot, Tyler and Matthew *(UK)*

Anouk *(Australia)*

María and Emiliano *(Mexico)*

Hardik and Aarush *(India)*

Philippe *(Russia)*

Jaelyn and Ana *(USA)*

Emanueli *(Brazil)*

Dóra *(Hungary)*

- The School Council and headteacher have got together and found ways to make our school eco-friendly. These small differences range from lights that turn off/on automatically, recycle bins and more.
  Evie, UK

- As Greta Thunberg said, our lives are in your hands. Because by the time we, the youngest generation, get into power, it will be too late.
  Freya, UK

- There will come a time when doctor's prescriptions will not be medicines, but would be to plant trees and take a walk in the woods.
  Mahi, India

- I can make sure that the lights are off in a room when I'm not in there. I can take shorter showers and not leave the water running.
  Saylah Mae, USA

- You could make a limit for using fossil fuels.
  Connor, USA

- There should be more chargers for electric cars around the country. I think that public transport should be cheaper.
  Jacob, UK

- In my village, during the summer time we receive much less rainwater than ever before. Everybody wants water, but they cannot get it because we have only one tank, but three other villages all rely on that same water from a single tank. Sometimes they all come to the tank and fight with each other over this water. I don't like to see people fight like this.
  Vipin, India

Dear children

The Global Sustainability Institute (GSI) at Anglia Ruskin University is celebrating its 10th anniversary. For our anniversary almost a hundred of you, each of you about the same age as our institute, wrote letters to World Leaders, sharing your thoughts about climate change and your hopes for the next 10 years. We received letters from children in the UK, India, USA, Australia, Russia, Hungary, Nigeria, Mexico, and Brazil.

In this book we have tried to bring together some of the things that have changed during your lifetime and highlight the things we need to do in the next 10 years – things that you call for in your letters.

Ten years is a lifetime for you, the children who wrote these letters. We have left it late, but not too late, to change our future. The next ten years are key.

Yours

Aled Jones

"To remedy the effects of climate change involves reducing the flow of heat-trapping greenhouse gases by reducing the burning of fossil fuels for electricity, heat or transport."

JASON
Nigeria

Climate change

Climate change seems to be affecting everything. So, what is it?

Pollution, often referred to as carbon emissions, from burning fossil fuels in our factories and cars, cutting down trees, agriculture, and waste, have collected in the atmosphere and act like a blanket warming up the planet. The last decade was almost one degree Celsius warmer than a hundred years ago. This warming across the planet puts a huge amount of energy into our weather system. So, while a slightly warmer planet melts ice and raises sea levels it also makes the extremes of our weather more likely and worse.

To combat climate change we need to stop emitting carbon as well as adapt to the impacts of the warming we are already experiencing.

Dóra, Hungary

"To me our Earth is a place full of contrasts. While there are some people who live in luxury, others barely even 'live'. They have to suffer a lot to make ends meet."

Impacts today: People

We are already seeing changes in our weather extremes around the world including droughts, floods, and fire because of climate change.

Over the rest of this century, temperature changes and rising sea levels, alongside more extreme weather events, will have big impacts on where and how we can live. Some countries will be more impacted than others but there is nowhere that won't be impacted. This will mean farming in some places will get more difficult, whole cities and towns will have to move and we will need to build our homes and places of work to be extra-resistant to the extreme weather events.

"Even though people see the problems caused by the destruction of nature, they keep cutting down trees, and this makes me feel very sad."

-Emanueli
Brazil

Impacts today: Plants & animals

The changes in weather (drought, flood, fire), and temperature will destroy the habitats of an uncountable number of the world's animals and plants.

In addition, our destruction of forests and the acidification of our oceans, where the oceans absorb some of the emissions from burning fossil fuels making them more sour, will add to this destruction.

Alongside other environmental pressures and pollution, we are facing the extinction of hundreds and thousands of plant and animal species around the world.

Fossil fuel needs to be replaced with cleaner, renewable energy like wind and solar power.

Aarush, India

Energy

We need to move much more quickly to a zero-carbon power system (a power system that does not emit any pollution) – more solar, wind, tidal and hydro power with energy storage everywhere. We need to make sure this energy system is cheap so that the poorest in our world have access to clean and affordable power.

What we have done in the last 10 years

- Solar installations increased, for example India saw a huge increase of 175 times – inventing a global industry for solar technology.
- We have doubled the amount of wind power that we have built worldwide – and its half as expensive.
- More than $500 billion is invested each year into climate change solutions.

What we need to do in the next 10 years

- We need to quadruple our investment to around $2 trillion per year to solve climate change.

I can help too. I can not use a car a lot and ride my bike. Ana, USA

Transport

We need to change our travelling habits to use more public transport, cycling and walking as well as move our vehicles over to electricity.

What we have done in the last 10 years

- Six million electric vehicles have been sold so far – effectively creating a whole new industry for electric cars, bicycles, and busses.

What we need to do in the next 10 years

- We need every new car to be electric.
- We need to fly less.
- We need to use more public transport, cycle more and walk more.

"I could plant lots of trees and help the worms because trees make air and worms help the soil."
~ Jaelyn, USA

Forests

We need to stop cutting down trees and instead plant more. We need to recognise the physical and mental health benefits that being in and near nature brings us.

What we have done in the last 10 years

- We have reduced the rate of deforestation by a third.
- People have shown what we can do if we collectively set our minds to it: In 2017 around 1.5 million volunteers planted more than sixty-six million trees in a record-breaking 12 hours, in the state of Madhya Pradesh, India.

What we need to do in the next 10 years

- We need to plant 1 trillion trees and stop deforestation altogether.

"We could support our local farmers"

Matthew, UK

Food

Food production generates huge amounts of emissions. Industry needs to change, and we need to change our diets to think less about low-carb and more about low-carbon. We need to ensure that our food supply chains can withstand shocks from extreme weather so that everyone can always access affordable and nutritious food.

What we have done in the last 10 years

- Sustainable food and farming initiatives have sprung up worldwide, showing what is possible.
- Between 2016 and 2018 there was nearly five times more orders of vegan takeaways in the UK.

What we need to do in the next 10 years

- We need to improve on this trend and eat even less meat.
- We need to change the way we farm to be much more sustainable and learn from local communities and farmers how to manage our soil and land better.

Philippe, Russia

"A strange thing is happening right now in Siberia. They report an extremely hot summer this year, up to 38 degree Celsius. This is not usual for people living in Siberia and they are not ready for that change."

Homes

We need to change our homes to be 'zero carbon', that means they should not add pressure on the atmosphere in the way they are built or lived in. We need to value houses as the homes they are - where our families live, grow up and flourish, not just as an investment to sell on to the highest bidder.

What we have done in the last 10 years

- Governments around the world have introduced support schemes for homes to install better insulation and renewable energy.

- A number of countries, like France and the UK, now require people to measure and report how energy efficient their homes are before they can sell them.

What we need to do in the next 10 years

- We need all our homes to generate their own renewable energy.

- We need all our homes to be well insulated, so they do not lose valuable heat in winter.

- We need our homes to be 'climate proof' – they need to be built to last, including not being built in places that will surely flood.

"Many crops fail and many people are starting to look for jobs outside the village."

HARDIK
India

Jobs

Jobs today are already being impacted by climate change. However, clean and renewable power will be a big employer of the future for this generation of children. We need to invest in the skills and training needed for the next generation to take advantage of this boom in 'green' jobs. There's huge opportunities for people to have a meaningful job in a greener world.

What we have done in the last 10 years

- Over 10 million people are employed in the renewables industry.

What we need to do in the next 10 years

- We need to support the massive jobs growth that will be seen in green sectors such as renewable energy.
- We need to invest in wider green skills across the economy to support the fast transition to zero-carbon.
- We need to support people to move away from coal and oil based 'brown sectors' through education, training and so called 'upskilling'.

Did you know that throughout history 1.42 trillion pieces of waste have been dumped into the ocean?
Tyler UK

Waste

We need to stop producing so much rubbish, recycle a lot more and change our products and the way we sell, so our products last longer and we can re-use more. However, we also need to recognise that at the moment waste is still the source of employment for millions of people around the world, and we need to make sure they find meaningful alternative work.

What we have done in the last 10 years

- 74 countries have banned plastic bags, including Nigeria.

What we need to do in the next 10 years

- We need to not only produce less plastic, we need to stop putting ten million tonnes of plastic waste in the oceans every year.
- We need to develop a circular economy where things are being reused as well as recycled.

"We are brothers who sometimes fight and we are learning to no longer fight and be a good team: do not mock each other, listen with respect."

María and Emiliano, Mexico

Behaviour

We all need to adopt low carbon lifestyles including changing how we consume electricity, how we travel and what we eat. We need more fairness in the world so the richest 10% do not contribute nearly half of all emissions.

What we have done in the last 10 years

- People around the world have started to understand what their own 'carbon footprint' is and change their behaviours to manage and reduce this.
- Villains in films and TV series including Thanos, James Bond and Dr Who are increasingly linked to climate change.

What we need to do in the next 10 years

- We all need to live within our own carbon footprint to make sure we, as individuals, are not overly contributing to climate change.

I hope more people will listen to First Nations people and have more respect for them and everyone will get treated equally because they know how to take care of nature and deal with bushfires

Anouk, Australia

Community

With the internet we are now more connected to each other around the world than ever before. However, on a real-life and local level, we are also more dis-connected than ever before. We need to prioritise our families, friends and communities instead of chasing the latest products; so we can maximise our wellbeing rather than just our wealth. We must value the things in society that make us happier - like love and creativity and try to do more of these – not value the creation of money above all else.

What we have done in the last 10 years

- A global community has been born – Facebook, Twitter, Instagram, Snapchat, Pinterest, TikTok.

What we need to do in the next 10 years

- We should change the way we work to give us all more time for our families and communities.
- We must value community knowledge and work together to create solutions.

"The power is in the hands of the leaders so act like one and save the world"
— Elliot, UK

Leadership

We need to have leaders at all levels of society that can respond to the challenge of climate change with bold and ambitious visions that inspire us all.

What we have done in the last 10 years

- The school strikes for climate were born.
- Governments have agreed to the Paris Agreement which pledges to keep temperature increases to well below 2 degrees Celsius.
- National laws have been passed with a commitment to reduce emissions with several countries adopting net zero targets including Sweden, UK, China and New Zealand.

What we need to do in the next 10 years

- We need a robust and ambitious international agreement.
- We need to put in place ambitious national policy to deliver real change that allows us to reach our emissions targets.
- Richer countries need to support others with access to technologies and money to help them respond and adapt to climate change.

Activity 1: Dear World Leaders

Below are a list of individuals, including a number of world leaders:

Prime Minister of the UK – The Prime Minister of the UK is elected every 5 years. The Prime Minister has a number of experts who help them decide what issues they feel are most important. In 2021, the UK is hosting a very important event called COP or 'Conference of the Parties'. Many of the world's leaders will visit the UK to discuss how the world is going to take action on **climate change**.

President of the USA – The President of the USA is elected every 4 years. The President of the USA is considered one of the most powerful political figures in the world. The USA is the world's second largest **producer of carbon emissions**.

President of the People's Republic of China – Over one-fifth of all the people in the world live in China. China is the largest **producer of carbon emissions** in the world. A lot of the products sold all around the world are made in China.

Greta Thunberg – Greta Thunberg is an environmental activist from Sweden. At age 15, she sat down outside the Swedish parliament with a sign that said: 'School Strike for Climate'. Her aim was to make politicians take action on climate change. On September 20th 2019, around 6 million people all over the world took part in a Global Strike for Climate.

- Think about who on this list has the most power to act.
- Organise the names into a list with 'most able to change our future' at the top, and 'least able to change our future' at the bottom.
- Are there other people you would add to the list?
- Discuss your list with your friends at school. Does everyone agree with your list? Why did some peoplc disagree?

Activity 2: What will the future look like?

The future of the world is not yet fixed. We have the collective power to change it. Find examples in the book of illustrations that show positive visions of what the world might look like in 10 years' time. Using these illustrations as inspiration, design a vision for where you live in 10 years' time. Use these questions to help you think about different parts of your vision.

- What will it look like?
- How will energy be generated?
- What sort of things will you buy?
- What will you eat?

Activity 3: How can you take action?

There are lots of organisations and people who are trying to help the world to become more sustainable. These are some ideas for ways that young people can take action.

Ways to take action:

Join a Youth Strike for Climate – These happen usually once a month on a Friday in cities around the world. Search 'Youth Strike for Climate' to find out about the nearest event to you, or consider setting one up locally in your school/youth group.

Start an Eco-Council at your school – Starting up an Eco-Council is a great way of helping your school to meet its own sustainability pledges. You could come up with a list of actions that you would like the school to take, and present these to your head teacher.

Write a letter to your World Leader and your local newspaper – World leaders have a huge responsibility to act. Writing to them shows that we care about the future and want it to be a safer, happier place for all. You could also write to your local government or a local newspaper.

Acknowledgements

This book would not have been possible without the letters we received from children around the world. We have not been able to reproduce them all here but would like to thank the children for sending us their letters. The letters can be read online here: **https://doi.org/10.25411/aru.14540628**

We would particularly like to thank the following primary schools:

- Garhwal English Medium School, Uttarakhand, India
- St Mary's School, Pune, India
- Stowting Primary School, Kent, UK
- Meridian Primary School, Cambridgeshire, UK
- Ling Moor Primary, Lincoln, UK
- Jeavons Wood Primary School, Cambridgeshire, UK
- Warren Elementary School, Ohio, USA
- Teresh Eternal Excellence School, Lagos State, Nigeria

We would also like to say a huge thanks to the BA illustration students at Anglia Ruskin University who gave their time to bring this book to life. A particular thank you to Allan Drummond at the Cambridge School of Art for all his support!

A thank you to the people who supported the work involved in bringing this book together including Nicola Walshe, Victoria Tait, Lauren Stabler, Felicity Clarke and Linda Gessner. Thanks to the team at the GSI (and their parents, friends and family members) who reached out to children and the schools above!

Special thanks to Lara, teacher and artist, who's insights and creativity infused this book with purpose and passion.

We are grateful to the ESRC Centre for the Understanding of Sustainable Prosperity for the funding that allowed this book to be published.

> We must listen first to nature, culture and indigenous voices that are working hard to leave the forest standing and then think of profit, because we are the land of the Amazon, we are every heart of every animal that goes extinct.
> Gabrielle, Brazil

> Rice is an essential part of our diet. Just a few years ago we could grow rice but now we aren't able, which makes it difficult for our families to get proper nutrition.
> Rajeev, India

> As I write this there are almost 100 flood warnings across the UK because of Storm Dennis, and yet my local city Cambridge is experiencing serious long-term drought.
> Emma, UK

> Cars use gas to power them but using too much has caused climate change.
> Ana, USA

> We want more: solar panels, water powered electricity, wind turbines and electric car chargers.
> Teddy, UK

> In the future the naturally produced bricks that the house is made of have microbes in them, to generate eco-friendly electricity, and the concrete holding them together has bacteria in, which makes the concrete heal itself when a crack appears, because of a chemical process that makes it form more crystals.
> Freya, UK

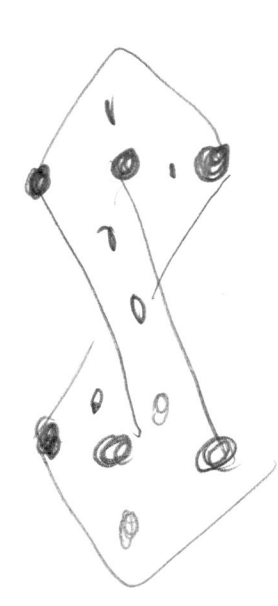

Aurielle

Printed in Great Britain
by Amazon